Mapping Global Issues

Immigrants and Refugees

Mapping Global Issues

Immigrants and Refugees

Cath Senker

A⁺

Smart Apple Media

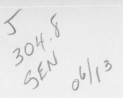

Published in the United States by Smart Apple Media
PO Box 3263, Mankato, Minnesota 56002

Series concept: Alex Woolf   Editor and picture researcher: Alex Woolf
Designer: Jane Hawkins   Map illustrator: Stefan Chabluk

Cataloging-in-Publication Data available from the Library of Congress
ISBN: 978-1-59920-509-0

Picture credits: Corbis: 7 (Ricki Rosen), 14–15 (Mike Hutchings/Reuters), 19 (Sophie Elbaz/Sygma), 22–23 (Sukree Sukplang/
X90021/Reuters), 27 (Richard Baker/In Pictures), 30–31 (Andrew Lichtenstein), 35 (David Turnley), 39 (Andrea Comas/Reuters),
41 (Andrew Holbrooke), 43 (Shannon Stapleton/Reuters). Shutterstock: 11 (Sam DCruz).

Cover picture: These African migrants are near the Short-Stay Immigration Center in Melilla, Morocco, waiting to find out
whether they will be granted permission to go to Spain, or will be sent back home.

The author would like to acknowledge the following main sources: '2009 Global Trends: Refugees, Asylum-Seekers, Returnees,
Internally Displaced and Stateless Persons' (UNHCR, 2010). *The Age of Migration* by Stephen Castles and Mark J Miller (Palgrave
MacMillan, 2009) Human Development Report 2009 (UNDP, 2009). *Immigrants: Your Country Needs Them* by Philippe Le Grain
(Abacus, 2007). *No-Nonsense Guide to International Migration* by Peter Stalker (New Internationalist, 2008)

Map sources: 9: *The Age of Migration: International Population Movements in the Modern World* by Stephen Castles and Mark J
Miller (Palgrave Macmillan, 2009); 13: UNHCR (2008) and IDMC (2008); 17: de Haas, Hein (2007). *The Myth of Invasion: Irregular
Migration from West Africa to the Maghreb and the European Union*. International Migration Institute, University of Oxford; 21: *The
Age of Migration: International Population Movements in the Modern World* by Stephen Castles and Mark J Miller (Palgrave Macmillan,
2009); 24: Based on figures from report 'Migration in the Asia-Pacific Region' by Graeme Hugo (GCIM, 2005); 29: *The Age of
Migration: International Population Movements in the Modern World* by Stephen Castles and Mark J Miller (Palgrave Macmillan, 2009);
33: HDR team data based on Ratha and Shaw (2006) and World Bank (2009b); 37: Based on figures in 'Population of Foreign
Citizens in the EU27 in 2008' (Eurostat, 2009).

Dollar figures indicate U.S. dollars unless otherwise noted.

Printed at CT, China.
SL001634US

PO1037
08-2011

9 8 7 6 5 4 3 2 1

Contents

People on the Move

Throughout history, people have migrated. This book explores the issue of migration in each continent, looking at why people migrate, where they go, and the positive and negative effects for the home and host countries. The focus is on migration between countries, although it is worth remembering that most migrants move within the borders of their own country. In 2009, approximately 200 million people lived outside their country of birth. They represented just 3 percent of the world's population.

Migration in Recent History

During the nineteenth century, a huge shift in population occurred. Fifty to sixty million people left Europe between 1800 and 1925 to seek new lives. The majority settled in North America, Australia, New Zealand, and Argentina. After World War II (1939–45), it was not only Europeans who were on the move. Asians, Africans, and Latin Americans migrated to the developed countries of the West. Since the 1980s, the process of globalization has widened the gap between rich and poor countries, leading to a rapid increase in migration to wealthier nations.

Who Migrates?

It is hardest for the poorest to move, even though they have the greatest reason to do so. They cannot save up enough money to travel and establish themselves in another land. People in the richest countries have the least need to move. Therefore, emigration is lower in the poorest and wealthiest countries than in those with moderate levels of development.

Wherever they come from, most international migrants are enterprising, adventurous people of working age; 45 percent are women. Permanent settlers, or immigrants, leave their country for good. Many others move temporarily rather than becoming immigrants. Temporary workers enter a country to do a particular job and then return home. Illegal workers enter a country without permission and remain hidden from the authorities. People may shift from one category to another. Sometimes, students overstay their visa and become illegal immigrants, while illegal immigrants might gain permission to stay in a country.

Forced Migration

Rather than choosing to move, some people are forced to migrate. Refugees escape from their countries because of war or persecution. In 2009, there were 14 million refugees worldwide, accounting for approximately 7 percent of international migration. An additional 26 million people had to abandon their homes and move to another part of their country. They are known as internally displaced persons (IDPs).

A Russian immigrant works on a production line making electronic registers in Israel.

PERSPECTIVES

MIGRATION

Migration is the oldest action against poverty. It selects those who most want help. It is good for the country to which they go; it helps break the equilibrium [balance] of poverty in the country from which they come. What is the perversity [unreasonableness] in the human soul that causes people to resist so obvious a good?

Canadian-born U.S. economist
J. K. Galbraith, 1979

Others are coerced into migrating by human traffickers. For example, in southern Vietnam, some parents are in such desperate poverty that they accept small payments in return for their daughters, who are then sold to brothels over the border in Cambodia.

Where Do Migrants Go and Why?

The increase in income inequality between developed and developing countries has made it more worthwhile to migrate from poor to rich countries. In addition, a decrease in the cost of transportation and communications has made it easier and cheaper to migrate. Most people move to a country in a similar category of development but with better living standards, although 35 percent of migration is from developing to developed countries. Even though migrants do not earn as much as local people, they will earn more than they would at home.

The majority of migrants select a place where they have contacts already—perhaps a relative lives in another country or there is a community from their homeland there. Migrants tend to cluster in the same geographical area and do the same type of job because friends or relatives in the host country introduce them to employers.

A Controversial Issue

Although the number of migrants from poor to rich countries has increased, migrants still form a small proportion of the population in those lands. Between 1960 and 2010, the percentage of migrants in developed countries rose from 5 percent to more than 12 percent. In the rest of the world, the proportion of foreign-born people is stable or decreasing. Nevertheless, migration causes great controversy, particularly in developed countries. While developing countries often permit low-skilled workers to enter on a temporary basis, developed countries tend to be more restrictive. They limit the number of migrants through immigration policies that favor skilled workers. These policies tend to bar low-skilled workers, even though there is plenty of work available for low-skilled migrants.

FACTS and FIGURES

WAGE GAPS BETWEEN NEIGHBORING COUNTRIES

- The average factory worker in the United States earns four times as much as a factory worker in Mexico and 30 times more than an agricultural worker in Mexico.

- An unskilled worker in Malaysia makes $100 a month but can earn $600 a month in Singapore.

- A factory worker takes home $250 a month in Poland but can make $800 to $900 a month picking asparagus in Germany.

Source: World Health Organization

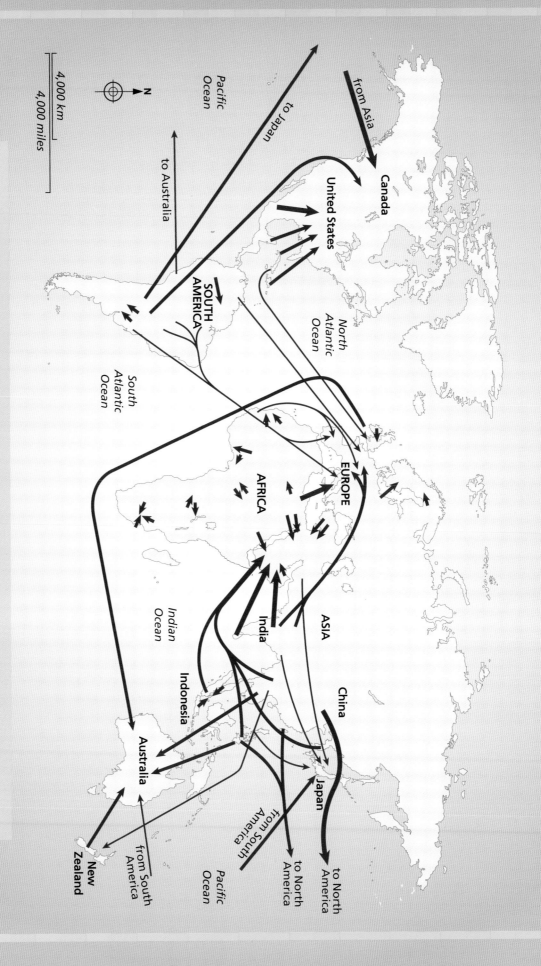

This map shows the main movement of migrants around the world since 1973. The thickness of the arrows gives an indication of the number of people who have moved. Thicker arrows indicate more people have migrated.

Sub-Saharan Africa

The majority of African migrants go to a neighboring land. Some migrate farther afield, sometimes to the country that once ruled their land as a colony. Others head for the European nations closest to Africa. Many Africans flee from conflict or economic crisis. This chapter looks at migration within and from sub-Saharan Africa, which is the area of the continent south of the Sahara desert.

Moving for Money

Most Africans migrate to improve their opportunities. The economic situation has caused a decline in income for many Africans, making it easier to leave. Since the 1980s, international organizations such as the World Bank have told African governments that to borrow more money, they first had to cut spending on health care, education, and administration. This has reduced the number of skilled jobs in these areas for educated people. Meanwhile, cheaper transportation and communications have made it more straightforward for people with money to travel.

However, most African countries are extremely poor. In 2010, Africa accounted for 33 of the world's 49 least developed countries. The majority of their inhabitants simply cannot afford to move abroad. Relatively few Africans—just 3 percent—live outside the country of their birth.

Forced Out

Millions of Africans living outside their home country did not choose to go but fled from conflict. For example, Somalia in East Africa has lacked a central government since 1991 and has experienced periodic fighting between rival groups for 20 years. In central Africa, the Democratic Republic of Congo (DRC) suffered a war from 1998 to 2003. Approximately 4 million people lost their lives, and fighting continues in the eastern region. Thirteen percent of international migrants from Africa move because of conflict—a larger proportion than in any other continent.

Some people leave to escape economic problems. For example, Zimbabwe suffers from a lack of political freedom, an economy in ruins, and high unemployment. Yet the government evicts people from their homes to prevent informal (unofficial) trading, which makes it extremely hard for them to earn a living.

PERSPECTIVES

MIXED REASONS FOR MIGRATION

A 42-year-old small trader, a widow with three children, tells her story:

When they destroyed my cottage and stopped us from working I had no money for food or rent or school fees. We slept under the sky in a riverbed for two weeks and my children all became sick and hungry. We went to live with my mother in the rural areas for three months. There was no work and almost no food. We only ate porridge and a little sadza [cooked corn meal] .... I left my children and tried for three weeks to sell vegetables ... but the police stopped me .... I came to South Africa in July 2006 to find food for my children.

From "Neighbors in Need"
(Human Rights Watch, June 18, 2008)

Refugees from the DRC crossed into Uganda in 2008. They left home with just the clothes on their backs and a few possessions.

Where Do Economic Migrants Go?

Most African migrants head for a nearby country with economic growth and a higher standard of living. They go to Libya, Ivory Coast, Ghana, and Gabon in the West or South Africa and Botswana in the South. West Africa is seen as the most mobile part of Africa. There are major movements from northern inland areas to southern coastal regions. Migrants move to take jobs in factories, mines, and plantations (large farms producing crops) or to work in the service sectors of large cities such as Lagos, Nigeria, and Dakar, Senegal. An increasing number of West Africans go further afield to Libya, South Africa, and Botswana. Some migrate to Europe, North America, Japan, or China.

South Africa, the wealthiest country of the continent, is attractive to economic migrants. Since the 1990s, migrants from as far away as Ghana, Nigeria, and the DRC have entered the country. Some qualified skilled workers and professionals have found employment in the formal sector (the official economy in which people pay tax on their income), while others have joined the ever-expanding informal sector—usually working for cash and not paying taxes.

Former colonial ties also influence where migrants go. It is easier for people to move to a country that has a link to their own. They usually speak the language of the colonial land. For instance, Belgium ruled the DRC from 1885 to 1960. Since the DRC became independent, some Congolese have migrated to Belgium. A 2010 survey showed that 40,000 Congolese had settled there. Similarly, Senegalese migrants have moved to France and Nigerians to the United Kingdom.

Increasingly, illegal African migrants arrive in European countries that have no colonial connections but are geographically close to Africa, especially Spain, the Canary Islands, Italy, and Malta. Although there is great alarm in Europe about these arrivals, fewer than 1 percent of Africans live in Europe.

Where Do Refugees Go?

Refugees usually have little choice but to head for the closest neighboring country. Political unrest in Zimbabwe has caused millions to flee—the majority to South Africa. Often, African countries that are in turmoil receive refugees from elsewhere. In 2003, conflict erupted in Darfur, western Sudan, displacing 2 million people from their homes and causing a mass exodus of refugees. In 2010, approximately 250,000 Sudanese were sheltered in neighboring Chad. Yet Sudan hosted more than 220,000 refugees from Eritrea, Chad, the DRC, and other countries. Likewise, in the same year, Ethiopia—which has endured conflict for decades and is one of the world's poorest countries—sheltered tens of thousands of Somali, Eritrean, and Sudanese refugees.

This map shows where wars in Africa have forced people to migrate. It indicates the conflict hotspots, major refugee flows, and the number of refugees in each country.

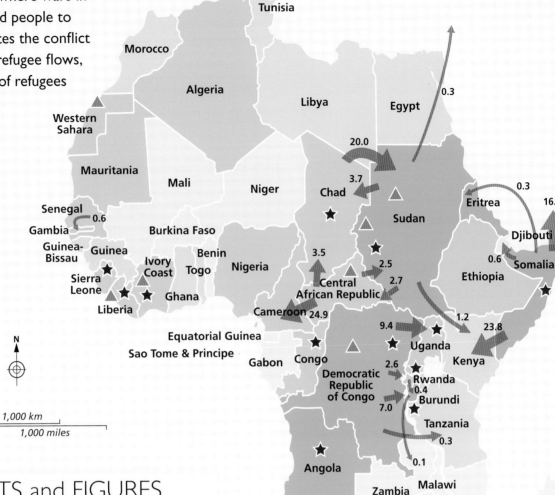

Tunisia
Morocco
Algeria
Libya
Egypt
Western Sahara
Mauritania
Mali
Niger
Chad
Sudan
Eritrea
Djibouti
Somalia
Ethiopia
Senegal
Gambia
Guinea-Bissau
Guinea
Burkina Faso
Benin
Togo
Nigeria
Ivory Coast
Sierra Leone
Liberia
Ghana
Cameroon
Central African Republic
Equatorial Guinea
Sao Tome & Principe
Gabon
Congo
Democratic Republic of Congo
Uganda
Kenya
Rwanda
Burundi
Tanzania
Angola
Zambia
Malawi
Mozambique
Zimbabwe
Madagascar
Namibia
Botswana
Swaziland
South Africa
Lesotho

0.3
20.0
3.7
0.3
16.6
0.6
3.5
2.5
2.7
24.9
1.2
9.4
23.8
2.6
0.4
7.0
0.3
0.1
0.6

N

1,000 km
1,000 miles

FACTS and FIGURES

NUMBERS OF REFUGEES IN AFRICA AT THE END OF 2009

REGION	REFUGEES
Central Africa and Great Lakes	969,300
East and Horn of Africa	813,100
Southern Africa	143,400
West Africa	149,000
TOTAL	2,074,800

Source: *2009 Global Trends: Refugees, Asylum-seekers, Returnees, Internally Displaced and Stateless Persons* (UNHCR)

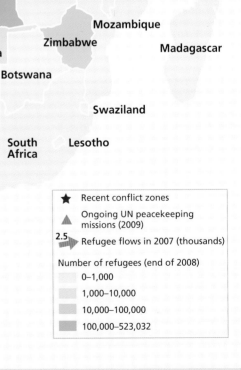

★ Recent conflict zones
▲ Ongoing UN peacekeeping missions (2009)
2.5 ➤ Refugee flows in 2007 (thousands)
Number of refugees (end of 2008)
0–1,000
1,000–10,000
10,000–100,000
100,000–523,032

How Does Migration Affect Home Countries?

Migration is often necessary, but it does have some negative effects. In Lesotho, approximately half of all married women have been left for long periods without their husbands. Some men leave for up to 15 years to work in South Africa. Their children may grow up without knowing their father.

The "brain drain"—when skilled and educated people in developing countries migrate and offer their talents elsewhere— is a significant problem. It is an especially serious issue in health care because so many African doctors and nurses move to developed countries. A 2005 report showed that more Malawian doctors were practicing in Manchester, UK, than in Malawi. African countries have a huge demand for health care—especially because of the deadly condition, AIDS. In 2008, 1.4 million people across the continent died from AIDS. Another 1.9 million became infected with the virus (HIV) that causes AIDS. Emigration has aggravated the dire shortage of health care workers in Africa.

Helping People Back Home

Migration also brings huge benefits. Remittances—money sent home by

Patients wait for treatment by overworked medical staff at a rural clinic near Lusikisiki in the Eastern Cape, South Africa. Doctors receive good training in South Africa, but many migrate for better jobs abroad.

DOCTOR SHORTAGE

Dr. Agyeman Akosa, the head of Ghana's health service, is in despair. "I have at least nine hospitals that have no doctor at all, and twenty hospitals with only one doctor looking after a whole district of 80,000 to 120,000 people," he says. Ghana, with only 6 doctors for every 100,000 people, has lost 30 percent of the doctors it has educated to the United States, Britain, Canada, and Australia.

From *Immigrants: Your Country Needs Them* by Philippe Le Grain (Abacus, 2007)

migrants to their families—provide an important source of income. According to the World Bank, migrants sent $10.8 billion back to Africa in 2007. At first, families spend the extra money on food and household basics. Then they improve their housing, invest in their children's education, and may buy land. Migrants also contribute to community projects in their homelands. For instance, Somali refugees in Minnesota often take on several jobs to make money. The local Somali coffee shops collect money from customers and send it via the mosque to their communities surviving in refugee camps in Kenya.

What Happens in Host Countries?

In host countries, the effects are mixed. When large numbers of migrants arrive within a short period of time, tensions can arise. In South Africa, hostility between local people and Zimbabweans resulted in an outbreak of violence in 2008. Mobs hunted down immigrants and raped, robbed, and murdered them. On the other hand, immigrants take the low-paid manual jobs that local people often do not want. In South Africa, migrants from Lesotho, Mozambique, and Swaziland work in the mines. Malawians and Zimbabweans labor as gardeners; Malawians and Swazi become domestic workers. Wherever they go, African migrants find a niche in the local economy.

The Middle East and North Africa

The Middle East and North Africa (MENA) region stretches from Morocco to the western border of Pakistan. Most countries are Arab states, but the area also includes Iran, Turkey, and Israel. Many MENA countries have the Muslim religion and culture in common, which aids migration within the region.

Migration within MENA includes the traditional movement of nomadic people and Muslim pilgrims going to Mecca; labor migration, either temporary or permanent; and refugees. This chapter examines migration within, to, and from MENA.

Israel, the sole Jewish state, encourages Jewish immigrants. As there are not enough workers for its economic needs, it relies on migrants from Romania, the Philippines, and Thailand. They come to this developed country to improve their living standards.

Migrating within MENA

The majority of migrants move for economic reasons. The Gulf States—Bahrain, Saudi Arabia, Oman, Kuwait, Qatar, and the United Arab Emirates (UAE)—are wealthy countries with extensive oil resources and strong economies. They attract many temporary migrants from Egypt, the Palestinian West Bank and Gaza Strip, Syria, and Jordan—places where there are not enough jobs for most of the young people in the population. Immigrants make up an astounding 80 percent of the population in Qatar and 70 percent in the UAE. As well as Middle Eastern workers, there are large numbers of migrants from South and Southeast Asia in the Gulf States

FACTS and FIGURES

REFUGEES IN THE MIDDLE EAST

In 2009, approximately 19 percent of the world's refugees were in the MENA region. They were mostly Iraqi.

Syria: 1,050,00 Iraqi refugees. Syria was the second largest hosting country in the world after Pakistan.

Iran: 1,070,500 refugees, almost all are Afghans.

Jordan: 450,800 Iraqi refugees.

2009 Global Trends: Refugees, Asylum-seekers, Returnees, Internally Displaced and Stateless Persons (UNHCR)

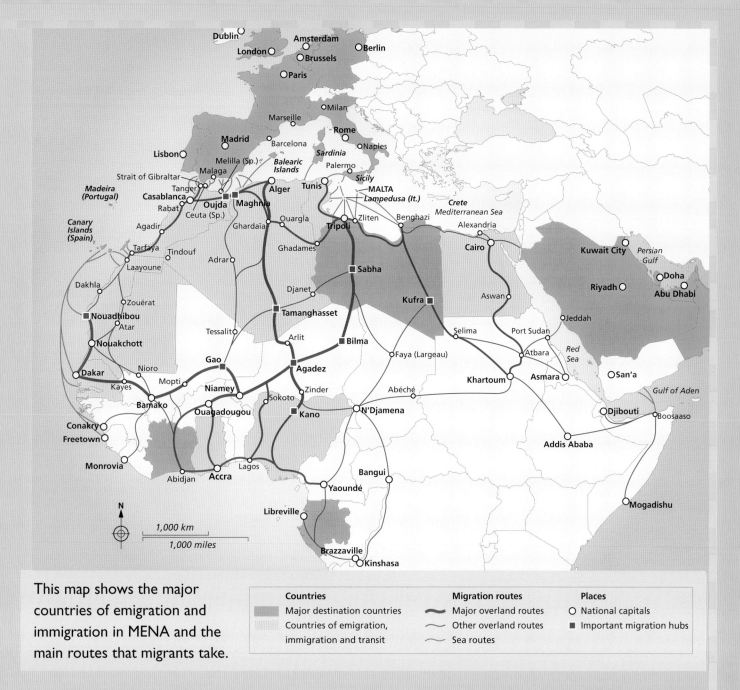

This map shows the major countries of emigration and immigration in MENA and the main routes that migrants take.

Countries
- Major destination countries
- Countries of emigration, immigration and transit

Migration routes
- Major overland routes
- Other overland routes
- Sea routes

Places
- O National capitals
- ■ Important migration hubs

Waves of Refugees

The existence of Israel in the middle of the Arab world is a source of political instability that has caused people to flee as refugees. Israel's establishment in 1948 caused the flight of 750,000 Palestinians. Most of their 4.8 million descendants (their children and grandchildren) still live in MENA with little hope of returning to Israel/Palestine.

Palestinians continue to leave the West Bank and Gaza Strip because of terrible economic conditions as well as the failure of the peace process with Israel.

The number of Iraqis leaving their country increased after the Gulf War of 1991. A second wave of refugees fled after the U.S.-led invasion of 2003. In 2009, there were 1.8 million Iraqi refugees, most sheltered in Syria and Jordan. In that year, Iran hosted 1.1 million refugees. Almost all were from Afghanistan, a country that has suffered invasion, occupation, and political instability for decades. Also, refugees from countries such as Ethiopia and Eritrea have found their way to nearby MENA countries such as Yemen. Overall, MENA hosted almost one-fifth of the world's refugees in 2009.

Emigration Outside the Region

Middle Eastern people also move outside MENA—especially to Europe, which is the closest developed region and can be reached without air travel. Connections have flourished between particular countries. Turks have been migrating to Germany since they were invited as guest workers in the 1970s. Moroccans, Algerians, and Tunisians have sought work in France, which used to rule their countries as colonies.

Sub-Saharan migrants pass through the MENA countries of Morocco, Libya, and Egypt to reach Europe. This is called transit migration. Some Africans do manage to enter Europe, but large numbers find it impossible because of strict immigration rules. They remain in a MENA country, and the transit country becomes their destination.

Migration: Negative or Positive?

Migration in MENA has various effects. On the negative side, some migrants, especially Asian workers, suffer poor treatment in the

Gulf States. An employer has to sponsor them by agreeing to employ them for a specific job. Some unscrupulous sponsors abuse the system. For example, they may confiscate workers' passports to prevent them from changing jobs. Others may treat their employees poorly.

Refugees also suffer hardship. For instance, Syria and Jordan are developing countries and have been generous in admitting Iraqi refugees. Yet the high numbers of refugees and a shortage of international aid have caused economic

These two young Filipino women had worked in the Gulf State of Kuwait. They escaped the violence and sexual advances of their employers and sought refuge at their country's embassy.

strain and led the Syrian and Jordanian governments to restrict refugees' rights. In Syria, Iraqi refugees have access to health care and education but cannot work legally. In Jordan, the majority of refugees have neither the right to work nor the right to use schools and hospitals. In 2006, Jordan closed its border to most Iraqi refugees.

Overall, however, migration has positive effects. MENA countries welcome emigration as a solution to unemployment and a source of remittances, which are particularly important to the economies of Morocco, Tunisia, and Algeria. The host countries also benefit. States such as Qatar and the UAE could not function without migrant labor. A United Nations Development Programme report in 2009 stated that "migrants boost economic output, at little or no cost to locals."

The Asia-Pacific Region

Asia is a continent on the move. Migration within Asia accounts for nearly one-fifth of all migration worldwide. Asian governments welcome temporary migration, although they do not generally allow permanent settlement. People choose to move within the region, to jobs in the Gulf States, or to Western countries. Some are forced to leave as refugees.

All kinds of people migrate. These range from the unskilled to top professionals and include a significant number of women. This chapter looks at migration within, to, and from Asia, including Australia but not the Middle East.

Why Do People Move?

As elsewhere, people migrate to carve out a better life in a richer country. Since the 1990s, the major growth of migration has been within Asia from the less developed countries to the newly industrializing countries. These are known as the tiger economies: Singapore, Taiwan, South Korea, and Hong Kong. Rapidly industrializing countries need labor for their factories as well as foreign professionals because their education systems cannot produce skilled people quickly enough. Although Asian countries rarely permit permanent migration, they make an exception for marriage migration. Women from poor backgrounds move to other Asian countries to marry men who are better off.

Conversely, Australia and New Zealand encourage permanent migration. Australia

FACTS and FIGURES

ASIAN MIGRANTS

- In the early twenty-first century, approximately 6.1 million Asians were employed outside their own countries within the Asian region, and 8.7 million worked in the Middle East.

- In 2005, there were at least 20 million Asian migrant workers worldwide.

- A large proportion of Asian migrants are female. In 2004, 81 percent of migrants from Indonesia were women. In 2006, women made up 72 percent of Filipino migrants.

    Source: World Health Organization

attracts many Asian immigrants as well as workers from Latin America, the countries of the former Soviet Union, the Middle East, and South Africa. All legal immigrants have the right to bring their family. In the early twenty-first century, Australia planned to boost immigration. New Zealand also has a substantial immigrant population, mostly from Asia and the Pacific.

Forced to Leave

In 2009, the Asia-Pacific region hosted more than one-third of the world's refugees, 75 percent of them Afghans. Three decades of conflict in Afghanistan have forced large numbers of refugees to shelter in neighboring Pakistan and Iran. These two countries host the largest refugee populations in the world. Asian lands also host refugees from other long-term conflicts in the region, including those in Tibet, Burma, and Sri Lanka. Human trafficking is a particular problem in Southeast Asia. An estimated 200,000 to 250,000 women and children are trafficked each year. Most are sold as sex workers.

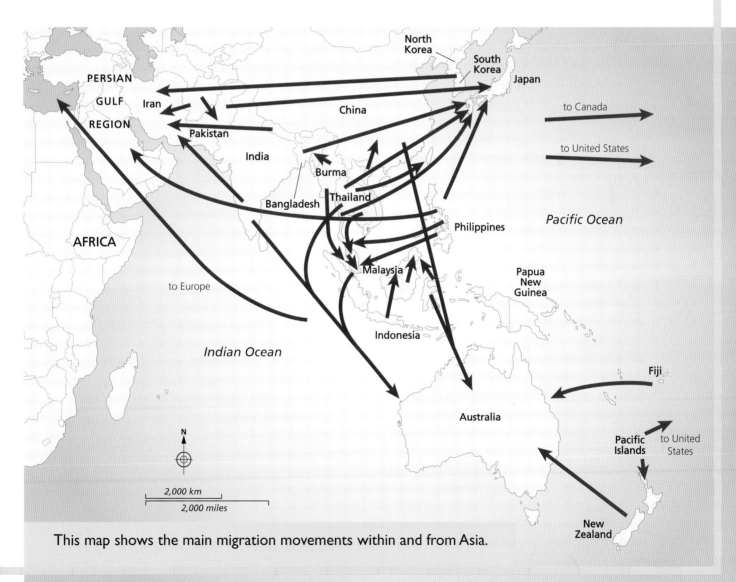

This map shows the main migration movements within and from Asia.

Where Do Workers Go?

All Asian countries have immigration and emigration. However, the balance varies depending on their economic situation. Wealthy countries such as Hong Kong, Japan, Singapore, South Korea, and Taiwan are mostly countries of immigration.

The countries mainly of emigration include Bangladesh, Burma, China, India, Indonesia, and Pakistan. Malaysia and Thailand have large numbers of immigrants and emigrants. Despite this movement, migrants make up a small proportion of the total labor force in many Asian countries— approximately 4 percent in East and Southeast Asia. In Singapore, however, the figure is 28 percent, and in Malaysia, it is 12 percent.

Jobs in countries with strong economies are at a premium, but would-be migrants may have no connections in their destination country. They may turn to a broker who can find a job for them and organize their paperwork and transportation, which is extremely expensive. Some migrants to Taiwan pay the vast sum of $5,000 to brokers for a job contract. Most people cannot afford

PERSPECTIVES

A CHINESE WOMAN GOES TO SOUTH KOREA TO MARRY

There were many people who went to work in Korea from my hometown. They became richer and built nice houses when they came back … I was keen to work in Korea. But it was quite difficult to get a working visa. One of my acquaintances introduced me to a Korean man. I just thought that I would marry him and as soon as I arrive[d] in Korea, I would run away from him and work somewhere. But the guy was quite gentle to me. We just fell in love with each other after several meetings …. But you have to know it, most foreign brides come to Korea because of poverty.

From "Marriage Migrant Women in Korea and Attempts to Organize Them" by Lee Inkyoung

the exorbitant fees, so they may take the risk of moving illegally. These migrants make their way from Indonesia and Thailand to Malaysia, but Thailand has many illegal workers, especially from Burma.

Where Do Migrant Brides Go?

Since the 1990s, more and more women have migrated for marriage. Again, they usually go to a richer country. Some journey from the Philippines, China, and South Korea to Japan. Others travel from Vietnam and Thailand to Taiwan. In China, farmers seek wives from Vietnam, Laos, and Burma. Marriage migration to South Korea is also on the rise. The brides, often young and poorly educated, must cope with moving to another country, where they do not speak the language and have no friends or family, to marry a person they have never met. These brave young women go to extraordinary lengths to improve their lives.

A migrant from the poor country of Burma works in a garment factory in Thailand. Employers in Thailand often ignore the labor laws and force employees to work long hours.

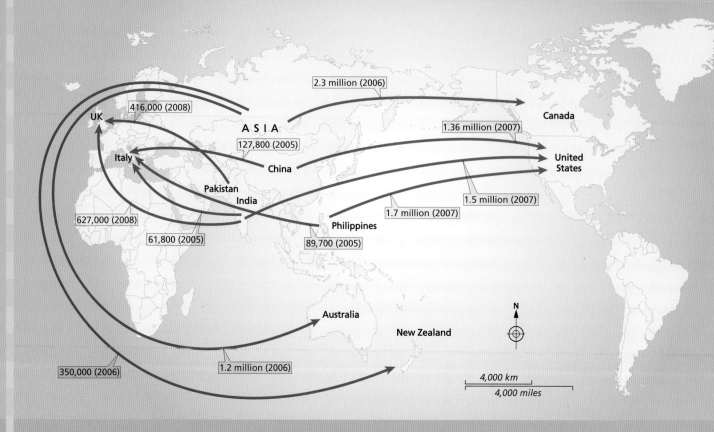

2.3 million (2006)

416,000 (2008)

UK

A S I A

127,800 (2005)

Canada

1.36 million (2007)

United States

Italy

China

Pakistan

India

1.5 million (2007)

627,000 (2008)

1.7 million (2007)

Philippines

61,800 (2005)

89,700 (2005)

Australia

New Zealand

N

350,000 (2006)

1.2 million (2006)

4,000 km

4,000 miles

This map indicates that Asian migrants have journeyed in large numbers across the world to Europe, North America, and Australia. The United States is the most popular destination country.

Going to the Gulf

Labor migration outside the Asia-Pacific region is also rising. Contract laborers, who are hired to do a specific job, travel to the oil-rich Gulf States. These countries are short of skilled workers as most local people work in the public sector (the government-run part of the economy).

The private sector, not under government control, depends on foreign labor. In the Gulf States, many foreign workers are low-skilled, but there are growing numbers of migrants in construction, managerial, and technical posts.

Long-Distance Migration

Some Asian migrants depart from the continent altogether, aiming for the United States, Canada, Australia, and New Zealand. Since 1992, people of Asian origin have made up about one-third of the immigrants to the United States. Family reunion accounts for a large proportion of the immigrants to these countries—people arrive to join families who have already settled abroad. The sources of migrants have become more diverse over the years. The number of Chinese migrants, in particular, has increased dramatically.

Who Is Welcome?

The United States, Canada, Australia, and New Zealand encourage skilled and business migrants from Asia. During the 1990s, half of all graduate migrants who arrived in the United States were Asian. The largest numbers came from India and China. Destination countries also welcome migrants who can care for their rapidly aging populations. For instance, nurses and caregivers from the Philippines go to the United States and Canada. In recent years, more Asians, especially from China, India, Japan, the Philippines, Vietnam, and Thailand, have started migrating to Europe. They include medical and information technology workers, female domestic workers (in southern Europe particularly), and manual workers.

Who Is Not Welcome?

Skilled workers are welcomed, yet despite the availability of jobs, developed countries restrict the entry of unskilled laborers. Therefore, these workers tend to be illegal migrants. Many go to extreme lengths to try to enter European countries. Some Chinese migrants pay smugglers to organize their passage across the Pacific locked in cargo containers on ships. Travelers pay up to $60,000 to a smuggler for a trip from Fujian, China, to the United States. Others choose the United Kingdom as their destination—it is slightly cheaper at $45,000.

Migrants may pay for this risky mode of passage with their lives. In June 2000, the bodies of 58 Chinese migrants were discovered in a container in Dover, England. Tragically, they had suffocated due to the lack of oxygen in the container. Despite the dangers, others still attempt to make similar journeys.

CASE STUDY

FROM SHANGHAI TO SEATTLE IN A METAL BOX

Crews removing a container in Seattle, USA, noticed it was lighter than it should have been if it were carrying 22 tons (20 t) of merchandise. A security officer noticed two men and a woman wandering around. Upon searching, guards rounded up a total of 18 men and four women. The stowaways had spent 15 days crossing the Pacific Ocean from Shanghai, China, in a metal cargo container. They had blankets, clothing, water and tools, and fans to disperse the air. Nevertheless, owing to the piles of uneaten food and containers full of human waste, the stench was terrible. The Chinese stowaways, in remarkably good health considering their ordeal, were taken into custody.

From "15 Days in a Metal Box to be Locked Up"
by Lornet Turnbull, Kristi Heim,
Sara Jean Green and Sanjay Bhatt
(*Seattle Times*, April 2006)

What Are the Effects of Migration?

For host countries, the efforts of migrants to reach their shores have several positive effects. Professionals fill vacancies at the top of the job ladder. For example, newly industrializing Singapore has recruited foreign professionals. Approximately 20 percent of its immigrants are doctors, teachers, or other highly skilled people. Immigrants also fill the gaps at the bottom rung of the employment ladder. Female migrants undertake childcare and domestic work, allowing women in the host country to pursue careers. In South Korea, local people do not want to undertake manual work, but migrants are prepared to work long hours for low pay in factories. In regions where settlement has continued for a long time, such as Australia, evidence shows that immigrants create as many jobs as they occupy.

There are downsides too. The vast numbers of refugees in Asia have created a challenge for governments, especially in Pakistan and Iran. Pakistan shelters the largest number of refugees in relation to its economic capacity and bears the heaviest cost when taking into account the size of its economy. Yet forced migration is just a small proportion of overall migration in the region. By the end of 2009, there were 3.9 million refugees in Asia. The continent hosted 61 million migrants in 2010.

Helpful to the Home Countries?

As in Africa, the loss of highly qualified Asian migrants has, in some cases, led to a brain drain in the homeland. Home countries sometimes suffer skill shortages and need to attract migrants. Taiwan, for example, is now trying to persuade emigrants to return.

However, in general, countries of emigration see the movement of workers as vital to their economies. Some countries, such as India, have surplus graduates. Emigration helps to reduce unemployment and provides workers with training and experience. Migration helps to reduce poverty too. For instance, in Andhra

PERSPECTIVES

THE BENEFITS OF SKILLED MIGRATION

Harinder Takhar, Indian migrant to Canada, community leader and Minister of Government Services from 2009, stated:

[Skilled migration] gives us access to a pool of talent not otherwise available. Half our engineers are foreign. They went to the very best schools. Thanks to them, productivity and quality are improved. It's a question of drive and sheer hard work. The construction industry in British Columbia is now owned by visible [non-white] immigrants. All taxi drivers and independent truck drivers are immigrants.

From *Immigrants: Your Country Needs Them* by Philippe Le Grain (Abacus, 2007)

Pradesh and Madhya Pradesh in India, the rate of poverty in a house with a migrant fell by about 50 percent between 2001–02 and 2006–07. A similar effect was found in Bangladesh. Overall, both host and home countries benefit from migration.

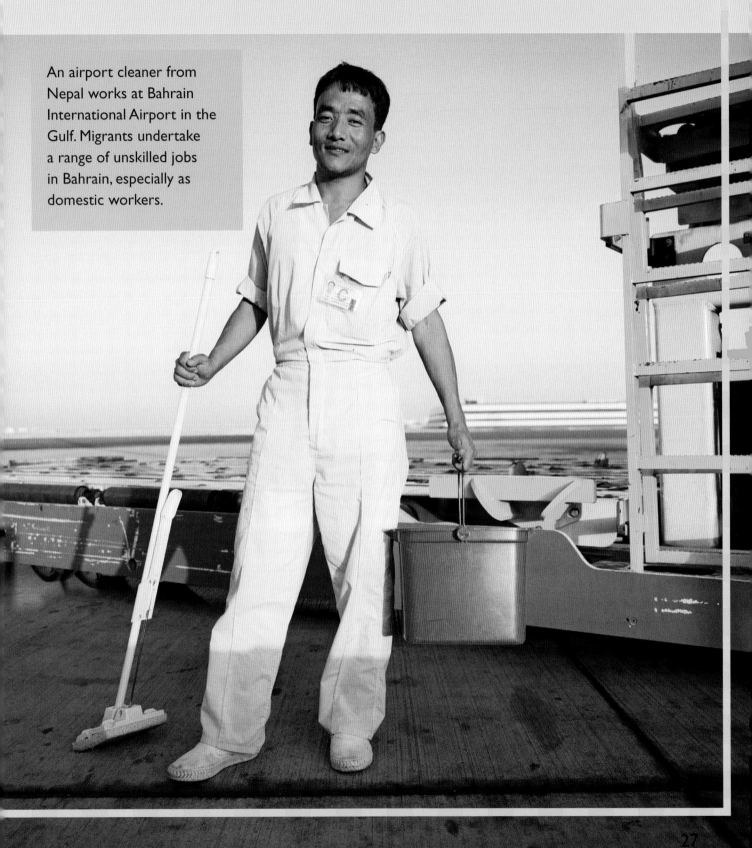

An airport cleaner from Nepal works at Bahrain International Airport in the Gulf. Migrants undertake a range of unskilled jobs in Bahrain, especially as domestic workers.

The Americas

The Americas include the developed nations of Canada and the United States and the developing countries of Latin America, including the Caribbean. Migration occurs between Latin American lands; some nations experience both immigration and emigration. Yet the trend is toward more migration to the richer northern American countries where living standards are higher. This chapter looks at migration within, to, and from the Americas.

Why Migrate?

Economic globalization has increased the inequality between the rich northern American countries and the poorer nations of Latin America. In Brazil, for example, the average wage in manufacturing in 2005 was $4.10 an hour. In the United States, it was $23.70—nearly six times higher. Even working in low-paying jobs in the United States, Brazilians can earn far more than they can at home. Economic crises, such as the one in Argentina from 2001 to 2003, have left a legacy of poverty and unemployment, creating a further incentive to migrate.

Being close to a rich country offers another good reason to migrate. Mexico is the poorer neighbor of the United States and provides almost a third of its total immigrants. Mexicans are frequently involved in circular migration. They go to work for a while in the United States and return to spend time in Mexico with their friends and family. Then they reenter the United States for another period of work. Some migrants from the Dominican Republic in the Caribbean take advantage of their closeness to Puerto Rico. They stay for a while, learning the

FACTS and FIGURES

FAMILY REUNIONS

- In 2008, 44.1 percent of new legal immigrants (lawful permanent residents) to the United States were immediate relatives of a U.S. citizen, and 20.5 percent were more distant relatives who came with a Family Preference visa.

- In Canada, 22.5 percent of immigrants in 2008 came under the family reunion program.

Source: World Health Organization

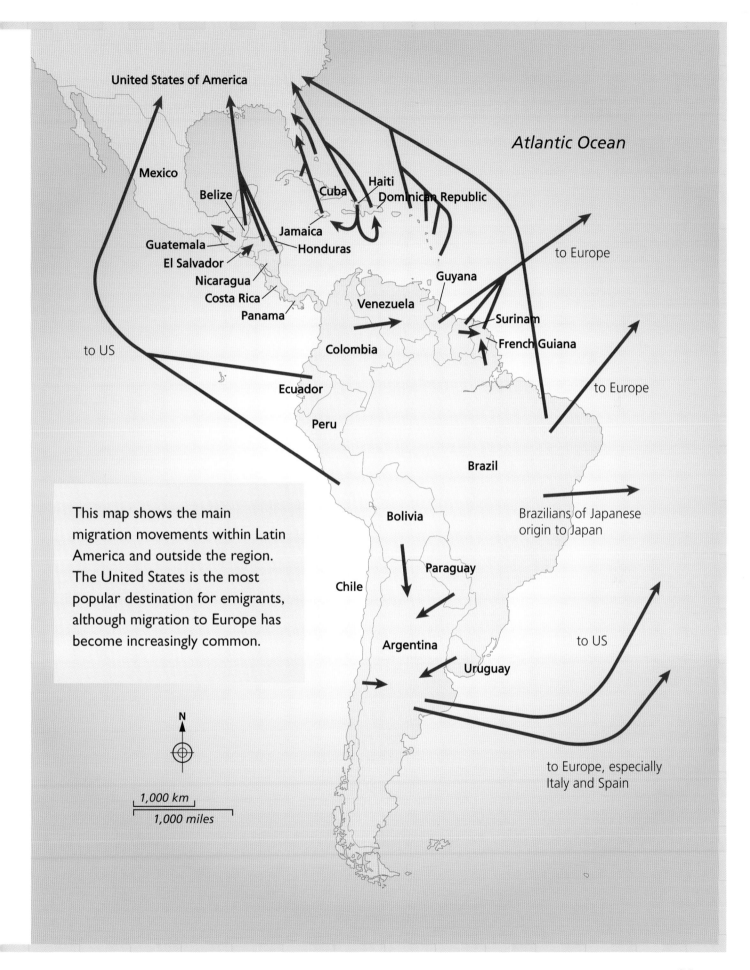

This map shows the main migration movements within Latin America and outside the region. The United States is the most popular destination for emigrants, although migration to Europe has become increasingly common.

local accent and buying false documents so they can pass as Puerto Ricans, who may freely enter the United States.

Refugees and Trafficking

The largest haven for refugees in the region is the United States, which hosted 275,000 refugees in 2009. The greatest numbers came from Iraq and Burma, but refugees from across the globe apply for admission to the country.

CASE STUDY

THE EXTREME RISKS OF MIGRATION

Inmer Omar Rivera, an electrician from Honduras, is desperate to reach the United States. Currently staying in a hostel for migrants in Ciudad Juárez, Mexico, Inmer traveled 2,000 km [1,250 miles] by train over 20 days to Mexico. Of the 2,000 who boarded the train initially, only 20 arrived. Relying on strangers to give them food, they ate on eight days alone. At military checkpoints, the migrants had to decide whether to jump off the train and wait for the next one or stay on and hide. Inmer was lucky. Sometimes he left the train and soldiers got on; other times, he remained and those who jumped off were caught. Many who jumped off died of their injuries. Having survived this extraordinary journey, Inmer fears being caught and sent back to Honduras.

From *Immigrants: Your Country Needs Them* by Philippe Le Grain (Abacus, 2007)

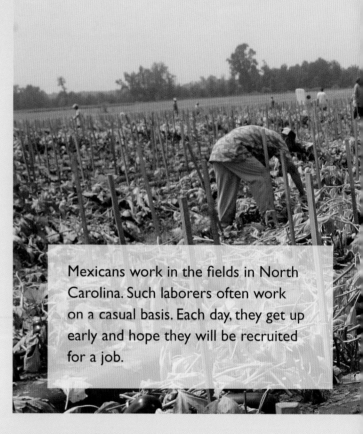

Mexicans work in the fields in North Carolina. Such laborers often work on a casual basis. Each day, they get up early and hope they will be recruited for a job.

The other main form of forced migration is people trafficking. In the early twenty-first century, there was a growing problem of trafficking from Latin America to the United States. A report in 2007 estimated that up to 17,500 people, including children, were trafficked to the United States annually. Latin American orphans and street children are vulnerable to trafficking because they often have no adult to watch out for them. They may be taken and sold as sex workers or domestic servants.

Which Destination?

Migration within Latin America remains important. Colombians move to oil-rich Venezuela, and people from various

countries go to Argentina, which is a country of both immigration and emigration. More than 65 percent of migrants are from other South American countries. However, increasing numbers of Argentinians are moving to the United States as well as Spain and Italy, which have special policies to allow them entry. Brazilians move to Portugal (which ruled Brazil as a colony), the United States, or Japan—along with other Latin Americans of Japanese origin.

The United States has experienced an upswing in non-European immigration, especially from Mexico, since 1970. Even though the United States restricts Mexican immigrants and forcefully polices the border, illegal migrants risk treacherous trips

through the desert in an attempt to sneak in. Canada is also a popular destination. It has a policy to admit the equivalent of 1 percent of its total population each year. Since Canada relaxed its immigration rules in the 1960s, more migrants have arrived from Asia, Africa, and the Middle East, rather than just from Europe as before.

What Work Do They Do?

Migrants' job opportunities depend on their country of origin, whether they are legal or illegal, and their level of skills. In Argentina, for instance, illegal migrants often work in domestic service, construction, textile factories, and agriculture.

The United States and Canada aim to attract professionals. For instance, the United States grants special visas to highly skilled applicants to fill posts for which there are no suitable local candidates. Yet the majority of migrants are in unskilled jobs. Mexicans are heavily employed in agriculture. California produces approximately one-quarter of the world's strawberries. The fruit is soft and must be harvested by hand rather than with machines. Farmers rely on Mexican immigrants for the job. Other migrants become health care or construction workers, nannies, cleaners, or taxi drivers.

How Are the Host Countries Affected?

In the United States and Canada, some people claim that immigrants take jobs from local people and cause wages to fall. Evidence from both countries shows that recent immigrants and the lowest-skilled people are the most likely to lose out from immigration. Yet immigrants often set up their own businesses and create job opportunities for local people.

In the United States, illegal migration is a major issue. Resources have been invested in the attempt to police the U.S.–Mexico border and prevent Mexicans and other Latin Americans from entering the United States. However, employers benefit from the flexible labor offered by illegal migrants. They can pay them less money, employ them when they are needed, and lay them off when they are no longer required. Migrants cannot complain about low pay or claim welfare benefits when they are out of work. They also have no health care insurance. Because they are not legally in the country, they have to remain hidden from the authorities to avoid being deported. Canada does not experience the same contradictory situation. It has a clearer immigration policy that aims to expand the population.

PERSPECTIVES

WINNERS AND LOSERS

The laws of supply and demand imply that, other things being equal, an increase in the number of low-skilled immigrants will lower the wages of comparable native workers, at least in the short run, because they now face stiffer competition in the labor market. In contrast, high-skilled workers may gain from the influx of immigrant labor. Not only will they pay less for the services these laborers provide, such as painting the house and mowing the lawn, but by hiring immigrant workers they will be able to specialize in producing the goods and services to which their skills are better suited.

George J. Borjas, U.S. campaigner against low-skilled immigration
(*National Review*, April 2006)

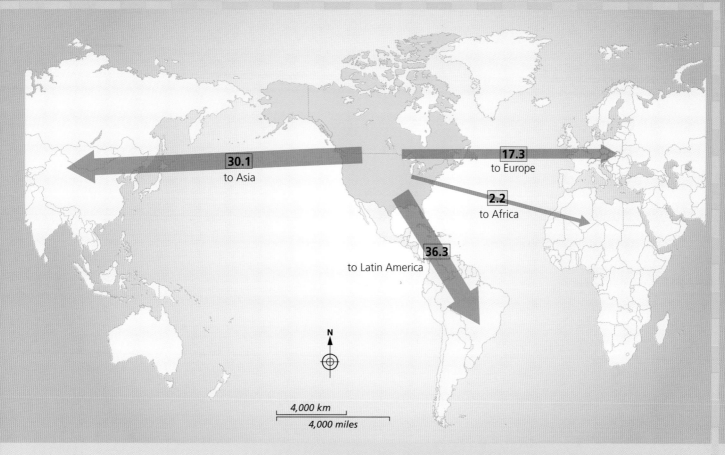

30.1
to Asia

17.3
to Europe

2.2
to Africa

36.3
to Latin America

N

4,000 km
4,000 miles

2.2   Remittances, 2006 (in $ billions)

This map shows the significance of remittance flows from North America to other regions. The thickness of the arrows indicates the size of the remittances.

What Happens in the Home Countries?

As elsewhere, remittances—mostly from the United States but also from Spain, Canada, and Italy—benefit migrants' families and communities in Latin America. These have a multiplier effect. For example, farmers back home use the funds to buy equipment and fertilizers that boost their output. They make more money, invest further, and create employment. Mexicans in the United States have hometown associations that support community activities in Mexico.

Migrants often return home and establish new businesses; this is common in the Dominican Republic. Yet, this can bring disadvantages too. When returning migrants buy land, this helps their families but may lead to a shortage of land for others. This problem has occurred in the Caribbean.

As in other regions, brain drain affects the countries of emigration and is a particular difficulty for small countries. In 2000, 80 percent of university-educated people in Guyana, Jamaica, and Haiti left to work in rich countries.

Europe

As one of the most developed regions of the world, Europe is a magnet for migrants. People come from other continents and Europeans from poorer countries migrate to the wealthier economies. Since the expansion of the European Union (EU) in 2004 and 2007, hundreds of thousands of eastern Europeans have headed for northern Europe. This chapter explains the major patterns of migration within, to, and from Europe.

Why Migrate to Europe?

The northern European economies are the richest and most attractive to migrants, while the southern regions have also developed strong economies and become countries of immigration. Migrants meet the expanding demand for skilled and low-skilled workers in the service sector, including health care, hotels, and catering. They fill posts in the informal sector, doing unofficial, casual jobs that are not taxed or monitored by the government.

In rich, industrial countries, many people are educated and reject manual work and unskilled jobs. Therefore, vacancies abound in low-wage sectors such as agriculture. For example, British farmers rely on fruit and vegetable pickers from eastern Europe. The workers undertake 12-hour shifts, every day of the week, for about $8 an hour. In developed countries, women with children often work. Families need childcare and help with the housework to make this possible. Latin American women, who speak Spanish, can find employment in Spanish households.

Poorly paid skilled jobs with long working hours and stressful conditions, such as nursing, prove unpopular among locals. Britain's National Health Service relies on migrant staff. In 2007-08, more than 60 percent of nurses and care workers in London were migrants.

Push Factors

Factors push people to migrate too. After 1989, the former Communist countries of Eastern Europe were transformed. Their governments no longer controlled the countries' economies, and people were free to set up businesses. Although new economic opportunities arose, Eastern Europeans were no longer guaranteed a basic level of public housing, education, and welfare. This led to greater inequality between those who benefited and those who lost out under the new economic conditions. An increase in unemployment led more people to consider migration.

People from outside the EU also migrate to take advantage of better economic opportunities. The differences in living standards between non-European and northern European countries are more stark than the divisions within the continent. Family reunion is another significant factor in migration, accounting for nearly three-fifths of legal immigration to the EU.

A laundry worker in an immigrant neighborhood of Paris, France. Although developed countries have growing requirements for skilled workers, many unskilled manual laborers are also required to serve society's needs.

FACTS and FIGURES

MIGRATION IN EUROPE

- Most of the population expansion in the EU during the first decade of the twenty-first century was due to migration.
- 56 percent of migrants in the EU are citizens of another European country.
- 75 percent of the EU's migrants live in Germany, Spain, the United Kingdom, France, and Italy.

Source: Eurostat, 2009

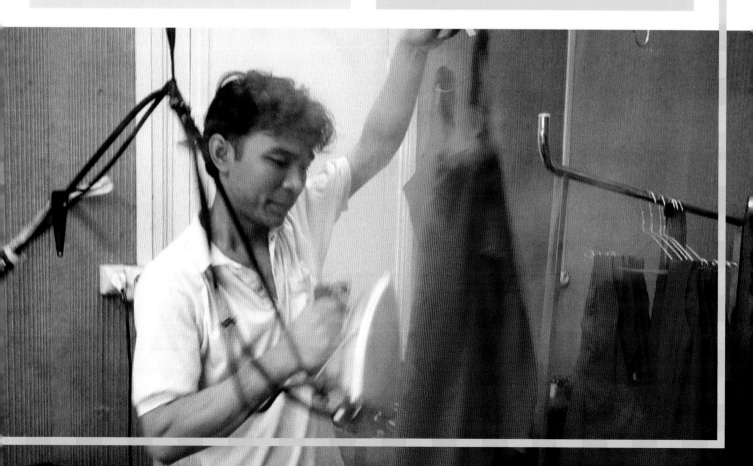

Where Do Migrants Go?

In 2004, the EU was enlarged to include 10 additional members, most of which were from Eastern Europe. In 2007, Romania and Bulgaria joined the union. In 2004, most of the 15 existing EU states restricted migration from the new member states. However, Ireland, the United Kingdom, and Sweden opened their doors to migrants. There were major influxes of Poles and people from the Baltic states (Estonia, Latvia, and Lithuania) to Ireland and the United Kingdom— although not to Sweden, which lacked good job opportunities at the time.

Other countries with many migrants are the wealthy nations of Germany, France, and Switzerland. Most migrants in Germany are Turkish, Italian, or Polish; those in France are Portuguese, Algerian, or Moroccan. In Switzerland, they are mainly European.

In the early twenty-first century, the southern European nations of Italy, Spain, Portugal, and Greece experienced an increase in migration. Romanians form the largest group in Spain and Italy. Spain has the largest Latin American population in Europe with more than 420,000 Ecuadorians and 280,000 Colombians as of 2008.

Illegals Take Risks

While some migrants, such as Latin Americans, are allowed to enter Spain and Italy, many other hopeful migrants, particularly from North Africa, have no legal option. They make difficult and dangerous journeys in the attempt to reach Mediterranean Europe illegally and often risk their lives in flimsy boats. Many would-be immigrants attempt the 60-mile (96-km) crossing from North Africa to Lanzarote or Fuerteventura in the Spanish-owned Canary Islands—a 20-hour rowing trip. Others take high-speed boats from Albania or Croatia to Italy. Since it is prohibited to transport migrants in this way, drivers may dump passengers overboard if they think they are likely to be caught by Italian customs officials. An estimated 2,000 people die each year crossing the Mediterranean Sea to Europe.

CASE STUDY

SURVIVING MIGRANT LIFE IN THE UNITED KINGDOM

To achieve the better life they yearn for, migrants often work overtime (extra hours), take on more than one job or frequently switch jobs, seeking higher pay. Mario, from Portugal, started off as a hotel waiter in Eastbourne, worked in a couple of glass and window factories, and later moved to London to work as a cleaner. But the job paid the minimum wage—the lowest legal wage—and the tasks were excessive. He was sacked [fired] for taking time off with a bad back. Mario then found work as a security guard, which he felt offered more opportunities. He hoped to progress to become a supervisor and improve his living standards.

From *Global Cities at Work* by Jane Wills, Kavita Datta, Yara Evans, Joanna Herbert, Jon May, and Cathy McIlwaine (Pluto, 2010)

N

500 km
500 miles

Iceland

Finland

Norway   Sweden

Estonia*

Latvia

Lithuania

Denmark

United
Kingdom*

Ireland

Poland

Netherlands

Germany

Belgium

Czech Republic

Slovakia

Austria

Hungary

Romania

France*

Slovenia

Bulgaria

Italy

Portugal

Spain

Greece*

Cyprus

Foreign-born population under 5% of total population

Foreign-born population between 5 and 10% of total population

Foreign-born population between 10 and 15% of total population

Foreign-born population over 15% of total population

* Data for this country has been estimated by Eurostat

This map shows the proportion of the population of European countries born in another country.

Emigration

As the media focuses on immigration—especially sensational stories of illegal immigrants—it is worth noting that Europe has a high level of emigration too. Foreign nationals leave and Europeans move to other countries. In Spain, for instance, the British formed the fourth largest group of nonnationals in 2008, while other Britons favored France, Australia, and New Zealand.

How Are Home Countries Affected?

Migrant workers in Europe can earn far higher incomes than in their homelands. Wages in Poland are typically one-fifth of those in the United Kingdom. Many Poles worked in the United Kingdom during the first decade of the twenty-first century then returned home with their savings. A downside was that Poland experienced a loss of skilled personnel, causing labor shortages during those years of mass emigration. For non-European migrants from developing countries, wages from even the lowest-paid jobs are sufficient to allow them to send remittances to their families.

What Happens in Host Countries?

Some observers argue that high levels of immigration create difficulties for host societies. They cite that large numbers of migrants arrive although many local people are out of work. They contend that if immigration stopped, unemployment would go down. Yet evidence from the United Kingdom and Ireland after the EU expansion in 2004 counters this argument. The new workers filled vacancies for skilled workers or took low-paid jobs that local people refused to do. There was no increase in unemployment or decrease in wages. During the economic downturn in 2008, fewer jobs were available, so fewer migrants moved to other countries for jobs. The number of eastern European workers registering to work in the United Kingdom during the first three months of 2008 was 25 percent lower than in the third quarter of 2007.

There also is concern about the number of illegal migrants. Even though governments have tried to restrict the entry of low-skilled migrants, there is still a demand for their labor, so they often come through illegal routes. Spain and Italy have tried to address this issue. Although most people arrive illegally or overstay their visas, many are legalized later and receive permission to remain in the country. Spain has attempted to work with African countries to reduce the

number of people making the hazardous journey. In 2008, Spain signed an agreement with Mali to allow the legal recruitment of workers. Arrangements such as this could help reduce the smuggling of migrants by allowing a legal entry route.

Some sub-Saharan African migrants try to reach Europe by traveling to Ceuta and Melilla, areas of Morocco ruled by Spain. These migrants are near the immigration center in Melilla, waiting to find out if they can stay or must return home.

The Outlook for the Future

A variety of factors will influence migration in the future. Economic circumstances will affect migrants' choice of destinations, as will demographic trends and the effects of climate change. Trade rules between countries can make a difference also. Immigration policies can make it easier or harder for people to migrate.

Economic Factors

In general, there will be more internal migration from rural to urban areas and from developing countries to the developed world. Migrants will still be drawn to the oil-rich countries of Saudi Arabia, UAE, Libya, and Venezuela.

In terms of regions, economic growth is likely to be strong in the Asia-Pacific region, so migration within the area will probably rise. Greater numbers of migrant workers could have social and political effects. Until now, Asian countries have promoted only temporary migration and resisted allowing migrants to stay permanently. This could change as they increasingly depend on migrants to do their "dirty, dangerous, and difficult" jobs and on professionals to fill gaps where there are skill shortages.

In Latin America, immigration to the United States and Canada will continue, and fewer migrants will travel between countries in Latin America. Immigration to Europe

is expected to expand too. Africans will migrate to wealthier parts of the continent, while greater numbers may attempt to reach Europe—depending upon restrictions imposed by European governments.

Demographic Trends

Changes in population will affect migration. Developed countries, in particular, have rapidly aging populations. Families are having fewer children, and people tend to live longer. This leads to a diminishing number of working people who can support the retired population. It is projected that the working-age population in the EU will fall by 16 percent between 2004 and 2050 as the proportion of people over 65 will increase by a dramatic 77 percent. Immigration can help to solve this problem and is likely to continue.

The world's population is aging and increasing rapidly. By 2050, it is predicted there will be more than 9 billion people—up

An Indian construction worker on a building site in Dubai in the United Arab Emirates. The Gulf States are likely to continue to be a magnet for migrant workers.

from 6.8 billion in 2010. Population growth puts pressure on resources and forces people to migrate.

Climate Change

Climate change—the gradual warming of the planet—is also an issue. Several regions of developing countries will be severely affected. For instance, parts of southern Africa are becoming drier, leading to longer periods with little rain. In contrast, increases

FACTS and FIGURES

POPULATION CHANGES

The projected percentage change in working-age populations between 2005 and 2020 if there is no net migration:

Japan	-11.6
Italy	-7.0
Germany	-6.2
Canada	-0.8
United Kingdom	0.3
France	0.5
United States	5.9

Source: International Migration Outlook, 2009

in sea level will lead to more flooding in coastal areas such as in Bangladesh. These changes are likely to lead to stronger pressure on people to migrate.

Refugees

The predicted disastrous effects of climate change, added to the frequent outbreak of wars across the world, may force more people to flee as refugees. Climate change, conflict, and forced migration are linked. For example, in Darfur, Sudan, rainfall has declined over the past half century. The desert is spreading. Arab nomads have less grazing land for their animals, and African and Arab settled farmers have less land and water for their farms. The competition between these groups for ever-decreasing resources has fanned the flames of conflict and pushed many to leave. The origins and destinations of refugees will shift, depending on where crises such as these occur.

What Can Be Done?

These challenges can be addressed. Measures could be adopted to reduce the effects of climate change in the most severly affected countries. Fairer trade between countries could allow people in poor countries to earn higher incomes for their produce so they do not feel the urge to leave. Economic policies, such as investing more in developing countries to create more jobs, could help narrow the gap between the rich and the poor countries.

CASE STUDY

FAIR TRADE BENEFITS

Oliva and her husband Joseph live in Uganda. They have seven children and four orphaned relatives to feed as well as school fees to pay. Everyone has to work hard. The family owns an organic coffee farm in Uganda. Oliva is responsible for the day-to-day running of the farm and helps to organize her local coffee cooperative. Joseph helps out and also has a job as an accountant. The children all work on the farm, weeding and picking coffee, feeding farm animals, and doing cooking and cleaning. Since the family is a member of a fair-trade cooperative, they receive a fair price for their coffee, fixed for the season. This allows them to budget and plan ahead with a sense of security. People like Oliva and Joseph have no need to migrate.

Source: Fairtrade Foundation, January 2007

Developed countries could change their immigration policies. Most need unskilled workers but try to bar them from entry. The workers still arrive but do so illegally. Some experts, including the United Nations Development Programme,advocate relaxing immigration controls and improving cooperation between home and host countries to regulate the flow of labor. They argue there should be more programs for people to migrate for seasonal work, such as in tourism and agriculture, and low-skilled workers should receive visas where their labor is required. Once they arrive, governments should protect their human rights, giving them decent working conditions and pay equal to what the local people earn for doing the same job.

Whether governments adopt these strategies or not, migration will continue as an integral element in our globalized world.

People will always be in search of a better life—and who can blame them?

In 2006, immigrants and their supporters demonstrated in New York for the right to remain in the country. States regularly pass laws to restrict illegal immigration, yet the lure of a better life continues to draw hopeful migrants.

Glossary

aid Food, shelter, or money that is given to people in need, such as after a war.

brain drain When skilled and educated people in developed countries migrate to work abroad.

brothel A house where people pay to have sex with prostitutes.

colonial Pertaining to the period when some powerful countries, especially in Europe, ruled other lands.

colony A region that is ruled by another country.

Communist An advocate of the system of government that existed in the Soviet Union and its Eastern European satellites, in which the government controlled the production of goods and the running of services.

contract laborer A worker who is taken on to do a particular job on a temporary basis.

demographic Relating to the changing number of births and deaths over a period of time.

developed countries Countries with a relatively high income per person where most people have a high standard of living. These include most European countries, the United States, Canada, Australia, New Zealand, and Japan.

developing countries Countries with a relatively low income per person where most people have a low standard of living. These include the countries of Africa, Asia (except Japan), Latin America, and the Caribbean.

emigration Leaving one's country to live elsewhere.

fair trade A system in which companies deal directly with producers and fix a fair price for a period of time.

family reunion A form of migration that allows family members to join a migrant in another country.

formal sector The official part of the economy in which people's jobs are recorded, and they pay tax to the government.

globalization A process by which countries around the world have become increasingly linked to each other through the rapid growth of trade, communications, and travel.

host country The country to which migrants move.

human trafficker A criminal who deceives people into leaving their own country; traffickers often sell these people or make them work as slaves.

illegal migrant A person who has entered a country in violation of immigration controls.

immigrant A person who migrates to live permanently in a foreign country.

informal sector Economic activity that is neither taxed nor monitored by the government.

labor migration Migrating for work.

Latin America The parts of the Americas south of the United States where Spanish and Portuguese are spoken.

net migration The number of migrants when the number of emigrants are subtracted from the numbers of immigrants. For example, if there are 200,000 immigrants and 100,000 emigrants, net migration is 100,000.

nomadic Moving from place to place in search of grazing land for animals.

occupation Moving into another country and taking control of it using military force.

pilgrim A person going on a religious journey.

private sector The part of the economy made up of businesses that aim to make a profit.

refugee A person who escapes to another country to seek refuge from war, natural disaster, or unfair treatment.

refugee camp A camp built by governments or international organizations to shelter large numbers of refugees.

remittance A transfer of money by a migrant working abroad to his or her home country.

service sector The part of the economy that provides services, including banking, transportation, schools, and hospitals.

sponsor An employer who agrees to take on a foreign worker to do a specific job.

transit country A country that migrants enter on their way to another country.

visa An endorsement in a passport giving that person permission to enter a country.

World Bank An international organization that lends money to developing countries and gives advice on economic policy.

Further Information

Books

Current Controversies: Immigration by Debra A. Miller (editor) (Greenhaven Press, 2010)

Immigration by Tom Lansford (editor) (Greenhaven Press, 2009)

In the News: Illegal Immigration and Amnesty: Open Borders and National Security by Janet Levy (Rosen Publishing, 2010)

Migration and Refugees by Cath Senker (Smart Apple Media, 2008)

How Much Should Immigration Be Restricted? by Andrew Langley (Heinemann, 2008)

Web Sites

www.iom.int/jahia/Jahia/about-migration/facts-and-figures/lang/en
This web site gives facts and figures about migration.

www.migrationinformation.org
This web site gives migration data from around the world.

pstalker.com/migration/
This web site is a guide to the history of migration, why and how people migrate, and the impact of migration.

www.refugeesinternational.org
The web site of Refugees International, a U.S. organization that helps refugees, provides links to information about current refugee crises.

http://www.unhcr.org/pages/49c3646c4d6.html
The UN Refugee Agency web site leads international action to safeguard the rights and well-being of refugees.

Index

Page numbers in **bold** refer to maps and photos.

The Student's Companion to Social Policy